my color

My Color

Savanah Stone

Published by Sacred Hearth Sage, 2022.

While every precaution has been taken in the preparation of this book, the publisher assumes no responsibility for errors or omissions, or for damages resulting from the use of the information contained herein.

MY COLOR

First edition. October 31, 2022.

Copyright © 2022 Savanah Stone.

ISBN: 979-8215842676

Written by Savanah Stone.

Table of Contents

For all the poets

Who will never get paid.

For all my humans

Who are afraid

of their voices

Because they don't know

what might come Out.

This is my whisper.

The words will yell for me.

This is to all the people who never let me jump without being a parachute.

This is for Vicki; wish you could've read this.

This book holds explicit content, please read carefully.

A memoir of poetry
By Savanah Stone

GRAYSCALE

Gray is my favorite Color. A grayscale actually. But the funny thing is, Gray
>Is not really a color at all.
>It's a shade.
>Black, white, gray
>and in between
>Don't exist in the rainbow. They exist to
>Darken
>Deepen
>Lighten
>Fade
>Strike
>Embolden
>All that we can see.
>Gray is not a color. It's the reality
>That life
>Isn't
>Black or white.
>It's a rainbow with different perspectives.
>It's a shadow with different hues.
>Different, not Wrong.
>Gray reminds
>me that everything has
>A reason,
>A season,
>A place
>In time
>To exist.
>Just, as, it, is.

SHADOWS - part 1

"This is the part where you run away." - Shrek

DISTRACT ME (art by Jess)

It's bad when you notice
    you're avoiding the place
    you are in

for a screen. Like,
I don't feel clean
trying to be me
so I sit
and stream another reality
and daydream.
The sad thing is
I came here to get away.
To prevent myself from staying home
alone,
and yet I feel the same.
I feel unknown
and unnamed.
Because what you would call me,
I don't want to hear it.
Or see it
or feel it
or believe it.
I just want to be.
So here I am, world,
what do you see?
What do you call me?
That's right, I know,
Afraid.
But where can I go
where loneliness
won't
Stay?

BARED TEETH

I get to be mad.
Yes, I *get* to be this time.
I get to be angry, because
no one's ever been mad
for me.
There's nothing to come clean about
except
to bring light to what you've
forgotten about.
That's me.
You left me here,
alone,
sad, and didn't even feel remorse. No,
you enjoyed
leaving me behind.
Know why? Him.
He was "true" and supposedly ensued to your cause. Your naive little
cause
to explore love.
I'm not buying.
Not trying to tell you to break it off.
No, he'll do that himself. And I will laugh
at your pain.
Yeah, it hurts
and I did tell you as much. But I guess his touch is just way too
intoxicating.
You know how I felt,
how I feel. Hell, you knew how she felt
and you still didn't care.
You tried to justify the wrong and kept coming up empty and bare.

So you bottled and exploded and hysteria and loaded insults and
cried.
All the while seeming to hide
from the obvious solution
to your stupid confusion.
You're not as great as what you think is on the surface.
And neither am I.
But now
I get to be indifferent. See,
you don't give wrath and expect to get sympathy back. You poor little
thing
who knows exactly what she does wrong
and still wants someone else
to fix it for her.
You're pathetic
and weak
and selfish
and pitiful.
I'm not mad about all that.
I'm mad
because despite everything
I said and will say,
you will still stay
in your unmoving grave
of procrastination.

HUMBLE

Can you see them shaking?

Smiles faking, Fingers aching, palms sweating from trying to grasp things they need to be getting.

Help.

Help is what is befitting to winning a life of choice. Help is what separates mental clarity

from the overwhelming noise.

Help is a lifeline some people see as toys

that they've always had. But for some people, help is not an option, seeking it is even bad.

Too expensive, too much attention, feeling like a helpless victim. Help will cost them more than their grocery bill, and their children have to eat.

Help would loose them too much

time they need to work

another job

or get barely enough sleep as it is.

Help is a witness to all the different privileges certain classes are blessed with. And you get distressed at the stupid decor of your therapist's office. Some depression is unmotivating, and some depression is safety stealing.

Some anxiety is distracting, some anxiety is starving

my fellow humans of any chance of leaving poverty. Money, racism, sexism, are just a few things fueling the income gap between

able to afford help

and not.

Let's stop talking about help like it's equal, because there's a lot that goes into being able to heal,

to stop,

to rest

and feel
all that our bodies carry.
The trauma
of our world is that our society barely cares
for those who can't care for themselves.
So,
we,
have,
to help.
Help those who can't help themselves.
Speak up
for the droves bogged down in hell.
The slaves to money
who never had a chance
to be anything else.
Let's give them
help.
Because none of us are free
until all of us
can breathe.
Let's find ways we can help, humbly.

DIVORCE

I'm trapped here, living in this dream, but I never wake up. I live here in this half reality, but it's never enough. You said you tried your best to make this friendship into love. But the only thing I felt you say was, hush.

How can you ask me to be somebody I'm not, when you get to be you? How do I know if anything you've said has ever been true? If you keep going and let me live like this then I can say...you're leaving me with no choice. I make no promises to stay.

How could you leave my heart in a corner, just to die? Didn't you know that all I had left was you, but that was a lie. If my soul was wrapped up in all of this time we spent between us, what did you think you were getting when you didn't put in work no one sees but us?

I was in it for real and I guess you could say, I'm a little bit numb. But even if no one else believes me or hears when I ask for someone to come- I will still know that without a doubt I did everything I could. And you just stood there-like I knew you would.

You said it was one-sided, but I couldn't disagree more. Because in the end love is pursuit and you never knew what you were fighting for. Not that I would call anything you did as close to a fight. But I would lie awake praying, hoping that it might.

You let me rot away like I was a corpse covered in mold. You thought if I had a smile on my face that you still had my hand to hold. Well I've got some news you didn't know. While you were so afraid of having no control, you never had any. You never listened. You left me frozen cold.

The point here is not to say if we did everything right. The point here is to say that yes, we're giving up, we lost the fight. The war was twice our lifetimes age and when I thought about it my heart cried. Because There's no way either one of us would've survived.

So when people ask me who's fault it was, I'll just look away and sigh. That's none of their business but if they must know then I'll tell them it was me who died. Because death do us part had no real meaning until I was alone. And learned what it means to be alone beside you in the house that wasn't a home.

Don't get me wrong I'm really glad that for you it was a good time. Neither one of us are perfect, and I won't forget your part in my life. But this morning waking up without you, the bed is cold at my side. While I might've shed a tear, I also smiled.

This is not the end of the story; this is not where my life ends. My life is beginning to look so fresh, regardless of the hurt and sin. Because I will fight til the day I die to find a better hope, a hope that denies misery and lets me breathe, lets me cope.

No matter how lonely I feel, I know you'll feel it more. That doesn't bring me joy to imagine, it makes my mind feel sore. Because at the end of the day though I'm walking away you're still one of my best friends. And this is where our story together ends.

Life is not a fairytale; we don't always get the girl. Life is not a carousel going in circles around the world. Life is not a movie where we get to win every time. Life is a stage with no cues or lines.

Treasures aren't found in boxes, maps don't outline your life's course. Love doesn't leave inside a day, doesn't always leave bitterness or remorse. I think of you every day, without a doubt, of course. But nothing is going to change that we're getting a divorce.

HAPPY BIRTHDAY

It's my birthday.
    Like thanks, it's supposed to be great
    but it's not. It's the worst day
    for hurt playing on my heart.
    Like it's a new year in my life to start
    trying to stop thinking
    about every reason
    today is anything but happy.
    It's not just the day I was born.
    It's the day I was torn apart.
    It's my divorceaversary.
    Because three years ago I sat
    in a courtroom and used a judge to get out
    of a relationship that abused me
    and refused to wait
    one more week
    or month
    for the possibility that it wouldn't happen.
    There was too much at stake to drag my feet
    or keep dreading. So I beat my lungs into submission to keep
breathing when he asked me
    if there was any reason why I should not
    be *allowe*d to divorce him.
    I trembled and looked at him,
    my fate on his ink pen and said the words,
    "No sir."
    So he said, "my judgment is sure and your divorce is official." Even
after the page was stamped and I had his dismissal I couldn't tell anyone
I lied.

How can I try to explain the divide that happened that day? The day he didn't show up

because he didn't have to.

The day I was throwing up in the bathroom

from accepting that the rooms I tried to build a home in were my failures.

Not gentle enough.

Not physical enough.

Not strong enough to push him away or scream. No. The only thing I did was retreat, dissociate and dream that I wasn't feeling anything.

That I wasn't there in my body.

That it was just discomfort

and that's a part of living.

How many times did my heart stop beating in that court room? How many people believed I was sinning for getting out of a house and relationship that was going to kill me?

How many did I hide my birthday from because it makes me so sad to remember

that it always rains in my heart.

Because I hate all my scars. And today,

on my birthday, they're fresh.

Believe me, sometimes

time doesn't let you forget

the rawness of the past. Sometimes pain

has a specific day it lasts

and lasts

and lingers

til my fingers are white and cold from clenched knuckles. Aching jaw, scrunched forehead. I'm not mad at you I promise. Just can't forget the memories

or anxiety

or need to hide my facial expression

inside of me. Because you really don't want
to know what I look like.
So that's why I appreciate it,
but don't wish me a happy birthday. Because
that kills me.
Please, just tell me instead,
it's going be okay.
You did everything you could.
And now you're safe
and healing
and living
and breathing
and that's enough.
You are enough, exactly as you are.
I'm proud of you
and you are loved.
In fact, let's all say that anyway. Everyday.
That's all anyone needs to hear us say.
And it's the only gift
I want on my birthday.

BETWEEN THE WALLS

(for all my trauma care workers, keep going)

Have you ever hated yourself?

Like really truly raging bashing eliminating everything good and positive and lovable about you in your mind?

Judge, jury and executioner delivering your sentence over and over and over in your mind- that, I, don't, matter.

That life is cruel and I deserved for it

to be even nastier to me. Because I'm worthless.

I hope you had a friend then.

A sister, a parent, an aunt, a passing stranger to tell you no. That's not true. That's a lie

that you can no longer hold.

But what if you didn't? What if all those people who were supposed to be in your life

weren't there?

Or they were dead or worse- they were the voices that told you those lies. What would you do?

What would keep you from your thoughts?

What would keep you from punishing yourself for not being enough? Not being perfect?

Not being who they want you to be?

Nothing. Nothing would keep you from the hate.

The unrest.

Nothing would tell you not to hurt yourself

for letting everyone down

even though it's just yourself you're mistreating. Nothing would keep you from that eraser rubbing, that pencil stabbing, that sharpener cutting.

No one would keep you from banging your head on the wall

to make the lies disappear.

The wall is immovable.
It's hard, solid, isolating. The wall doesn't listen
or judge your actions. It simply is
as you break yourself apart on it.
But we care.
We know that your voices inside are lying. We know the truth about you. That life is worth living. That brokenness is most beautiful, uncovered. That darkness will pass and morning does come. That love is worth the painful parts. And that if you have to be worthy of it,
it isn't real love. Real love is worth fighting for.
So we bring truth to you. You who are unable
to understand the lies yet.
The walls don't hear your head banging. We do.
The wall doesn't feel your depression and anger and hopelessness. We do.
The walls don't feel you head thudding again and again. We do.
We put ourselves between you and the wall. It's my hand you hit to keep from hurting your head. It's us you insult to drive everyone away. We stay, so your heart isn't sealed alone. The walls don't hear your mother's unacceptance, your father's abuse.
But we do.
The walls can't keep you from hurting yourself.
So we do. The walls don't care
if you give yourself a concussion.
The walls could care less if you are alive.
The walls are silent.
The walls let you decide
how much your head will hurt.
We don't.
We are between the walls.
We know the truth about who you are.
We know the lies you believe.

And even if you can't see them yet,
We will protect you.

SECOND RELAPSE

Be okay.
You *have* to be okay.
Because this isn't about you- it's about him!
He's the one broken.
He's the one throwing up and cold and sweaty and remorseful.
But what about you?
What *about* you?
Me.
I have feelings too.
I am affected too.
I am here and hurt and let down and disappointed and lied to
and
asked to forgive.
Again.
And again. And again. And again.
When will I say
stop.
When will I actually let go?
What's worse: a lie to get out of the woods,
or a truth to pull us in further?
Going through the woods once or twice.
What's worse?
I couldn't say.
All I know is
I have to be
okay.

SOMETIMES

Sometimes the face in the mirror isn't mine.

Sometimes, I find their eyes look different over time. Like someone hurt them or told them lies. Someone screamed and made them cry. Someone never asked why they so much like to hide.

But I'm asking. Looking at myself like

what *is* happening? When we retreat, is it really the best option or a habit? Matter of fact, it probably was easier to find other reasons to leave and let go, rather than stay behind and wait to find the courage that we're sometimes, too weak to reach for and take. To save ourselves from silence and the violence when we stay locked up in our own head. To just live until the day the

dam of our mouth breaks open and we say everything.

It's okay. I'm fine. I'm not good, I'm not great.

It isn't fate that haunts my every dream, my periphery, my own debates.

It's the tapes that keep getting played over and over in my brain. I can't stop them sometimes, but I'll tell you what they say.

"I wait, for the day the failures ruin our name.

I wait, for the depression to finally drive us insane. Down the road of a dead end without a coldisack. And we just go straight.

I wait, for the anxiety to take all our energy and drain our will to stop and examine all the beliefs that exist more like chains or handcuffs rather than jewelry."

How I wish the filing cabinet full of my thoughts was something that even sometimes looked pretty. Not the jumbled mess of crumpled paper that home my regrets. Or the discarded, mainly blank pages that remind me of ideas I was always too tired or overwhelmed to really make into dreams, let alone reality.

"I wait, for the day my brain is not the disorganized place that my OCD tendencies don't make anxiety.

I wait, for creativity to be something I could maybe get paid for. Because it's the only vocation I would do for myself and receive joy with the check, not just an energy deficit.

I wait, for the wreck of my body to stop convulsing on its own when I try to fall asleep. Because it remembers to be vigilant, you never know what's out there.

I wait, for when my cat dies. The endless tears I'll sob. The absense of her purr when I awake from a night terror. I won't know where I am again, because she won't be soft beside my head taking up most of the pillow. Licking my face when I didn't know I had cried."

Sometimes, the tapes are louder than my concentration. So I sit constipated in my mind from thoughts that just won't pass no matter how hard I push.

"I wait for the day my brain stops feeling like mush."

IF YOU KNEW

This was it. The third time. The last time. Your relapses were conditional to us. Us, like we mattered to you.

But despite what you said, we didn't.

Because here we are. On the other side of your choices.

Your failures.

My hurt.

Because this time

When you blacked out into alcohol.

Into oblivion

You left your reason behind.

What I was to find

As we quarantined together

Me, out of my mind

In agony

Being faced with believing that

I was never enough

Or worth being enough

For your effort.

On top of that

Waiting for a negative test

So you could get out

Go get help

At your third rehab.

I was a fool to not listen to the red flags of your past.

In our trapped suffering

Of waiting

Your hopeless, failed self

Made a choice I never thought you capable of.

You assaulted me.

But it wasn't you.

It was him.
The demon inside of yourself
You let him take over
In intoxication
So you could momentarily
Not be you
Not feel anything.
And he made me feel everything
I had tried to forget
To erase
To make healed.
He tore it open
He insisted upon his way.
He broke me
In a new way.
A way I had thought
not possible.
Because how could I possibly break more?
How could a rape survivor find anything more horrible. How foolish
I was
To tempt life with that challenge.
Because you knew my past.
So somehow
It was so much worse
When he tried to have his way.
And now I'm here. Waiting
For a new insurgence to kick in
So I can begin again.
And again.
And again and again.
Restitching my soul.
Listening to my heart.

Apologizing to my body.
Reestablishing safe
In myself.
I wonder how long it will take
This time.
And you blacked out.
So you have no memory or idea
Of the moment my illusion of home
detonated.
I wonder what would be different if you knew.
But I loved you.
All of you.
Until your flames almost finished me. I had to remove you before I
disintegrated into dust.
No. You don't need to know.
You don't need to burden
Yourself with another failure.
Another reason to hate yourself.
I forgive you
For giving me a wound I can't forget
I can't remove myself
I can't afford therapy
But I will heal
Probably
with one more invisible scar
Eventually.

PROCESSING

Sitting. Waiting.
　　For what?
　　Who knows.
　　For the grass to grow,
　　For the snow to fall,
　　For the trees to moan,
　　For the birds to call,
　　For my eyes to see,
　　what you did to me,
　　For my mouth to say,
　　what you did today,
　　For my brain to decide,
　　whether to leave or stay.
　　NO. This is *my* house.
　　For the rain to stop,
　　For the boot to drop,
　　For my heart to bleed out,
　　or better, just stop.
　　NO. This is *your* problem.
　　For my patience to die,
　　For the weariness inside,
　　to come out and swallow me whole.
　　It isn't like I have to deal with this behavior everyday,
　　right?
　　For my scream to feel the air,
　　For you to be more scared,
　　of losing yourself
　　over losing me.
　　Because really,
　　you already have.

For the glass to break,
For the wind to take,
my sighs away with it.
For the moon to come out and watch me.
Don't you understand what this cost me?
For the soul to recede
from the border between
you and I.
For you to realize
you won't die from this.
No. You will survive this.
You *will* survive this.
Like the last time
and the next time,
you will stay alive
long enough to remember.
This isn't the end.
The end of us
is not the end of you.
Or me.

SOON

And just like that
    He's gone. Finally
    Off to rehab
    For another chance
    For his brain
    To reset
    And heal
    And think
    And pray.
    I wish I was going to rehab
    To wash out these lies that have
    Clung to me
    For days.
    You weren't enough
    Or Worth it.
    You weren't
    A good enough reason.
    You
    Weren't
    Good enough
    For him.
    Or anyone.
    I sigh. Two more tears.
    But that's all.
    He knew this was the last chance.
    He knew he had already been given grace from the last time.
    He knew all the reasons he was already breaking my heart.
    And still
    Didn't care enough.
    Wasn't intentional enough

To meet my needs.
No more
Will I think about
A future with him.
No more
Will I rely on his presence
To soothe my anxieties.
No more
Will I ignore the needs of my soul
Or distract myself
With someone else's problems.
I am alone
With God.
They assure me.
"I am with you.
I am sorry it came to this.
Let's rebuild your boundaries.
Let's build bridges of hope and
Love and
Connection.
No more do We
Allow you to hurt here.
Get up.
It will be okay.
Not yet. But
Soon."

ADDICTION

Just one more.

But I can't do this anymore.

I know.

Just one more rep. One more plate and glass.

Just one more

Then we're done.

Just one more drink one more hit one more chance you give to them. Just one more time. Just one more snooze one more episode one more fight one more slot and stub. One more kiss bite hug squeeze laugh smile.

Just one more step on this journey of believing the lies of dopamine.

Please. STOP.

Just one more shift one more call taste hit. Just one more dance rave wild crave until I stop

Giving in.

Just one more thought I've chosen to rot this broken feeling hopeless and lost wondering

What all the one mores cost me.

Just one more, is a toxic boasting that everything I've loathed has control

Over my decisions and recognition

Of when one more, is too much.

Just one more day of coasting by

The silent weeping in my heart.

Just one more tear will eventually dry,

Right?

Just one more night lying awake in bed

Afraid of all the things you said would one day

Pile over my head and suffocate me.

As if it already hasn't.

Just one more piece of paper and plastic.

One more tree sacrificed to the god of wastefulness and greed.

One more sea creature strangled.

One more child starving

One more alarming article

One more potential wasted in a society that doesn't value the hard work it takes to raise a family

Or just a single life with joy.

Just one more gift one more smile wink one more stop and stay awhile. One more drink shot bill don't stop til you drop dead. One more time I get to say

I love you.

Because maybe

It really is the last.

One more moment alone with each other.

One more hands intertwining like the vines that grew over the old people's garden.

Because love was something they tended to.

One more second we believe is worth something instead of nothing.

Just one more slate piled up by procrastination you never get around to washing clean.

Just one more hour we refused to be wasted.

One more step in the race where we chased our face to erase all the pain we could see.

Just one more human I could ruin looking back at me waiting for whatever words I could let come out of my mouth.

One more refusal to let judgment keep me

From forgiving them. The reflection in the mirror.

One more blink one more bath to wash away the attachments we've come so far to build.

One more day in this life.

One more way we consume to survive.

Just...

One...
More... NO.
You
Have tortured me
Long enough.
I'm done giving up on my sanity.
I will not abandon me any longer
No matter how strong my habit is.
I choose
To live.
And I will give whatever it takes
To end
This addiction.

SUNLIGHT - part 2

"All we have to decide is what to do with the time that is given to us." - Gandalf

AT LAST

I sit alone on a park bench. Dirty.

Everything is dirty. The river had flooded and brought sediment above wooden bridges and benches. So now I sit on the dirtiness, exhausted.

We broke up in a messy dramatic ending
Where he chose the drink over my company.
I sigh, remembering it all and I hear IT say to me
"At last
We are here.
We've been excited for
This moment
Forever."
"This moment," I respond,
"Is the most hopeless,
Lonely,
And dismaying point
I've ever been to. YOU know that's saying a lot."
"Yes,"
They say,
"This is the moment We will build from.
At last we are here
In the dirtiness
On a park bench
With the whole world in front of us."
"Where will we go?" I ask Them,
The Eternal Moment.
"Wherever we want."

ART IN MY BLOOD

Creativity is in my cell membranes. Forget blood, there's art beating through my heart. It's in my DNA and it goes way back.

Art is in my mom, who worked hard for independence since she could drive and started driving other students to school on a bus when she was sixteen. Stick shift, no CDL. I wonder if she knew then about the three degrees she would achieve, completing on the art of teaching others. After having kids. There was art in the burn that came when cancer said, no, you can't teach anymore. The flames of healing like a sculptor's chisel. The loveliness when she knew one day she would be finished with chipping away the excess cells she didn't need, and get to say yes again to getting to stand in front of a whiteboard or screen and teach art appreciation. Because no one knows how to appreciate life more than her. Especially considering her cancer-free situation.

Art is in my grandmother who spent her life making her American dream come true; creating a family and caring for others. My Gran made art out of looking after every small person given into her arms. She made discipline beautiful, and fun intricate like music. She played with every child like each smile was a brush on a canvas of love in her existence. She spent years doing everything she could for others, selflessly painting a picture that reality is never about you, it's about us. I'm so glad I get to be in her picture. So grateful for every ounce of her love.

Art is in my paternal grandmother as well. She raised a family proudly, guitars and singing all around. You could tell by her gentleness and faith, she had treasure in life so profound. She became a widow when I was five, but her songs were not unsung. She lived grateful for her family, her sons, her grandchildren. She did all she could to be generous. There was art when she heard the call of the woods in her favorite place. As old as she was, she was fearless and followed her dream to live in a place outside of a city and enjoy her days in peace. Waking to sunshine, walking outside, living and loving her fullest life.

There was art in my great-grandmother too. She could play the piano until the day she passed away at 96. She also specialized in the art of cutting hair. But really, she explore the art of giving other women confidence and courage to start again. Her fingers didn't just touch follicles, they touched souls. When she was finished, you could see more of the person underneath. You felt known.

Art isn't just the thing with notes or colors. It's the subtle, sensitive, muddled, delicate energies, of finding your joy in the world that feeds into others. It's loving what you can give as if there's no other possible place you could be than just being here with each other. It's remembering all the mothers and grandmothers and great-grandmothers before us that showed us how to paint with our hearts, sing with our brains, and take our hands to make the world a better place. So make your mamas proud and share art with whoever can see your face. Love and be loved like it will never be erased. May art forever flow through your veins.

THE BEGINNING

I used to hate the night. Like

if things could be just a little bit brighter, it would be alright. But life would grow dim. So I prepared for a fight with myself again. One I knew

I wouldn't win. Colors would fade

and shades of gray crept in. My eyes would adjust, but my heart didn't budge. The darkening of our world was a nudge,

reminding me of everything that remains

in the dark.

The hidden things I starved. The memories that only creep back to myself when the sky is stark. When the reds carve their way across the expanse

and the moon moves to replace the sun. The shadows that jump and lunge and taunt

like they weren't just images.

The helplessness that I couldn't control. Lack of witnesses I needed the most. The weeping that no one could've saved me in my own home.

The terror of dreams I had no choice but to feel and see and hear. At night I was afraid. Because so many times no one was near and

it was too late. In the darkness

there was danger I couldn't evade...

But one day, I stopped. In my blackened room alone, just sat down and rocked. Back and forth. Until my heart sighed and whispered,

"No, No More...Please, no more."

I was so tired. But my mind was wired. So I knelt down, face to the ground and let go of it all. I let control fall away and accepted it. Stopped drowning the pain and rawness to start feeling it. Every. Single. Moment.

Every place that was broken. To the last shiver and sob. I didn't know if I would survive. Because I lived it. Again. And again. Until there was no power left given to a time that doesn't exist anymore.

Collapsed on the floor, my crying turned to smiling. My grieving into laughing. My laying into dancing. Because the beautiful thing I began to realize about night, was that it was never the end of the day. There is evening and then there is morning. Darkness doesn't have to be the end of the story. We aren't sentenced

to our worst fears getting energy and glory.

We are given the opportunity to sit with them and look them in the eye and forgive them.

With no one by our side, safe in the dark,

held and hidden by shadows, souls ripping apart, we are given space to choose love.

To choose another day, another ending for the mess we remember. Especially

when we feel nothing at all.

Night gives us a choice to reflect.

It is the perfect beginning to intercept.

No greatness, or strength came out of weakness and pain without sitting in the dark.

So slow down,

settle in,

be silent,

breathe in.

And out.

Breathe in all the tension and restlessness.

Exhale the exhaustion, regret,

and release yourself of the responsibility

of making up for

what was taken from you.

Let what's lost be a reminder. Not of why it hurts, but that you, are still, here.

Do not just fear, but also Think

and rest

and sleep
and wake up.
Get dressed for what's waiting for us.
Light is always there at the end.
Stop worrying if the darkness wins.
There was no competition to begin with.
It's only a friend
teaching us how to release the tragedies
and reach for truth.
Night is not evil,
and neither are we.
Hope isn't found by ignoring the things
that bind our hearts and spirits.
Hope is finding light at the end of the day,
not the beginning.

MUSIC (for Grandaddy)

You know that tune?
  The one you can't get out of your head?
  That one. Right there.
  You smiled because you remembered.
  The music is like a conversation. How we're all good. Maybe a little
rowdy.
  But mischief is holy
  and we dance
  because we can.
  I am inspired because I can't help but be. Included in the symphony
  of passion and revelry that rolls
  deep below our skin. Beating,
  singing back

that we're alive.

SUNRISE

Light creeps s l o w l y
    Pooling into the sky.
    Laaaaaaaazy.
    Deliberate, Intentional, Sensual.
    Like you'll never see it
    This way again. So you better look
    Closer.
    PAY ATTENTION. Be
    Here and nowhere else.
    She is inviting
    You to wonder.
    Explore. Get lost. Stop wanting
    To be found.
    Let the soft playground
    Embrace you, care for you.
    Hide you.
    Momma Earth
    Teach your wisdom, fun, faith, beauty, Love.
    If only you would go
    And stop moving
    So far away.
    "Be here," She insists. "Don't take our intimacy from me any longer.
I want to enjoy your presence.
    My Daughter.
    My Son.
    My Everything.
    Me."

THE CALL

"Come be with me, come be with me,"
Mountains kindly insist.
"How"
I ask. They reply,
"By saying yes. Yes now and
Always."
"I seek you out
Star Whisperer
Sacred
Sage
Hearth.
My soul is the flame that
Sits restless, powerful, content, protected.
Finally and
Forever
Home. Into the wide beyond of my gaze, Living.
Because I exist only as a perception,
particular, specific
Inside
All that could be
Experienced.

ARE

You are the God who changes hearts, not I.
    You are the God who sings us songs
    and teaches us to remember
    how to breathe.
    You are the God who taught the cobra to strike, the lion to pounce,
    and my mind how to overcome fear.
    You are the God that runs with pumas,
    flies with Eagles, swims with sharks,
    and has individual love for every
    single creation imaginable.
    You are the God who has never run
    from anything,
    but makes others tremble with a breath.
    You are the lover who put passion in our hearts, valiance on our
tongues, and justice in our minds.
    You are the God of redemption.
    You are the God who tells the wind to play in our hair and
encourages us
    to take the leap and let you catch us.
    You are the God who does not sleep
    but desires the deepest rest for our souls.
    You are the God who is the mastermind
    of the universe, but never tears us from control of our free will.
    You are the God who did not want robots
    as people, you wanted love
    that comes from choice,
    commitment, hard work, and endurance.
    You are the God that will walk with me
    no matter how dark the past,
    dangerous the climate,

no matter how longing are my betrayer eyes.
You are the God that sees me
for all I am,
all that I've done,
all that I will continue to do
in the nastiness of my own way
and will not look away.
You are the God of melodies that tell the truth about the beauty in
the world
and how gross it all can be.
You are the God of reality; the one who can makes dreams true, the
laws of physics move, and your greatest dream was us.
We are the children of God.
We are the conquerors of soul death.
We have the right to speak up,
not to remain silent.
Because that is what evil would love,
but it can't keep us quiet. It can't tell my heart something it doesn't
believe.
It can't tell my soul that I am the reason
for my own existence.
It can't tell my mind God doesn't make sense because that's the whole
point!
Love does not make sense to humanity!
What a beautiful thing to realize.
No matter how distant, no matter how gruesome, no matter how
terrible we can be, God's greatest desire is for all to know Them
and know Their love.
Don't you dare want to believe anything else.
I want to see Love move in your life. And when I look at anything
other than God
I have stopped moving towards the person I am going to become.

You Love, are the God who lives in us.

We are full in your fullness. We are taught inside your wholeness and complete among your infinity.

Return to us
the desperation
to heal in your presence. Be the warmth
on my back when the sun won't shine.
Be the hand in my own
when no one is around.
Be the gentle breath
that rekindles fire in my soul.
Let the words I speak
and the meditations of my mind
be pleasing in your sight.
Oh Love, my strength and Redeemer.

STAGE FRIGHT

I want to be here. I do.

    That's so clear in my mind.

    It took a lot of time, thought and energy

    to write down these lines that I love,

    and I'm proud of. It's not that I'm worried

    if they don't make sense. I really couldn't care less. No, what stresses me out

    is this.

    Being right here, in front of everyone. Open.

    In the sight of God, you, your friends. I can't unsee your emotions. And,

    I can't stop caring.

    I can't win.

    But I belong on this stage.

    The platform is worthy of the art on my pages

    I can bring to it. But I'm not.

    That's all it comes down to. The words are marvelous, beautiful, and true. But me?

    I'm nobody. I'm not important.

    I live on the borders, staying in corners

    so I can watch the room. Scared of the moment someone notices, of the looks that loom.

    I hide in my books. The stories I create

    are just another way for me to run away and escape.

    What am I so afraid of? What is keeping me from stepping freely in the bravery

    I would much rather be known for?

    Poems will be forgotten one day. I'll die and rot and float away into stardust

    when the sun explodes. I only trust that

there is absolutely no real control or certainty.

I wonder if hope is just the universe's way to humor me into living. Into giving

so much of myself and planning to live forever.

If I can't count on tomorrow, or even today,

is it fair to say- there's no point to fear

except to keep us alive? Can I make it clear

to my shaking heart that it's alright

to get up on quaking knees and do something hard that's so, easy. Take a breath,

open my mouth,

and speak.

Tell everyone listening that as depressed as I am, there are things that deserve our beliefs, attention and direction.

There is compassion worth feeling,

people waiting for our affection,

sunsets begging for reflection.

There's a whole world out there waiting for us. There are people and relationships

in your life who you love and return the sentiment. Adventures and wonder and whimsy to ponder, get worked up into a frenzy to experience the freedom of joy

in right now. Each moment could be anything you want. Choose to start again. Be your own best friend. Decide to win. Be the captain of your release of monotony into peace

in being present.

I have so much I want to say to you,

listener.

So I have to stop feeling hesitant.

Darkness and lightness in life need to be spoken. These words have chosen my busy mind,

my broken heart,

my cheap pen to become real through.
Who am I to question them?
I have to get up and tell you what they say.
Send me courage. This is going to be a long day and night of fighting my weak resolve.
But I don't have to solve this alone.
I made it here.
I'm not at home on my couch like I could be.
I guess I'm growing in humility from being in a lime light.
And maybe one day
I'll get over this stage fright.

CHRISTMAS MAGIC

Christmas day used to come with such wonder.

It was magical, exciting, anticipatory.

Then we got older.

We learned

how to be petty.

We saw the presents instead of the tree.

We saw the food instead of the feast

of company.

The magic disappeared.

Crept away from us, one day just gone. Like

getting older had stolen the wonder and whimsy, leaving us greedy
and empty.

A shame. But there are some who look again. They don't give up with
the hopelessness.

They stare at the symbols.

They remember how to be childlike.

They dream. And they find

what they're looking for.

The star becomes a beacon. The carols, reverent pledges. The tree, a
hope in victory. The gifts, a royal reminder. We were not left forgotten by
a cold universe. We were found

with mysteries of humility, integrity and sacrifice. Christmas magic
is born again in the honor and celebration of freedom. So next time

you wish Christmas felt like when you were a kid- go deeper.

Understand the magic is only the beginning

of a truth that waits for you in maturity.

UNAFRAID

Do you ever get scared of your fear?

Like, you feel it, it's here. Waiting for the day

you let your guard down. Turn off the surround sound on your speakers and headphones.

It watches when you're home alone. It lingers. Uncurls its fingers. Getting ready to grab your lungs, squeeze your chest, so you, can't, breathe...You try your best to shake it off,

you're not weak. Groan and cough like it's a sickness you caught from someone else.

But who are you kidding? It's been attached to you like a wedding ring- take it off and feel the sting. Like you cheated. Said "I do" to too many misleading untruths. Lies that stay far away

from any logical sense anyone would say.

So you stay distracted by elaborate contraptions designed to steal your focus, your time, your life. Misery, apathy, safety become your wife. What a bitch she really is. Restitching the clothes you should've thrown away a long time ago.

But you didn't. Those linens are comfortable.

Why try something new when you don't actually know if it'll fit better on you? So you stay glued to the tv, the shows, the podcasts, the hoes of attention that society won't overthrow

but accepts. There are no interventions

for living a dissatisfying life. But what if there were? What if we turned to her, that fear

we placate who keeps us dazed and engaged in the inner pettiness and said no. What if we let go of our own throats and sat down with ourselves? Stop putting lies onto our head's shelves

and drowned in our eyes. What would we see? What would be staring back at me?

Anger, sadness? Screaming. Madness? Thrashing against all the feelings that just want to be seen and felt. To be noticed and held and listened to like they mattered. What if you let them wash over you, battered your heart like a wave

of faith and truth. What if instead of sinking,

you floated to the top and the lies dropped

into oblivion. What if thinking about all the things that scared you gave you clues?

About what's old and dead, or new and deadly? What if you stopped dreading stillness and said yes to silence? To trying to find rightness

in what your fear is telling you. What if you let

the right things break you and realized it's okay

to shatter. Because maybe those pieces didn't really matter, and weren't a part of you anyway.

Next time you feel fear's claws at your neck,

tell her to hold on a sec. Grab your nail clippers and a file so you can take care of her and she can stay a while. Listen to her needs so you both can become free from each other and have some space. Maybe you'll start to see less and less resemblance in your face and feel at home right where you are in this place. Finally, unafraid.

I have a vague memory
of my mother holding
me on a cold
night.
I was warm and safe,
Like a Blanket.

SACRED TOUCH

Do you know what it's like to hide?
Bide your time... skirt to corners,
the borders of the room.
Forfeit the middle things
for the most little, defendable position. To listen...for the footsteps
of the people you're avoiding.
Do you know how it digs a void in the center
of your being?
Showing anyone would be a bother, annoying.
It hurts.
This distance between you
and the rest of the world.
Toying with you, taunting. You won't risk it. Crossing that space into
the inside,
away from the divide of
separateness.
Your body craves a touch, a hug, any sort of physical form of love.
To remind you, that you are real.
You forget how it feels to be held, without
the obligation to pull away.
That embrace you can just
stay
still,
just, as, you, are. And rest.
Why is it so hard to decompress?
Why? Because you're depressed and anxious.
A reminder of the memories that arrest
your mind and constrict your breathing.
You'll never be able to forget bleeding
from those misunderstanding people

who chose to hurt you instead of dealing
with their own wounds.
Who made your bed a hard place to be, terrifying really. The night
terrors are almost gone,
but so is the integral hope,
that you will never be alone.
In this darkness, enters a hand. A gentle
caress that pulls you close. But you can't breathe.
What if they see me?
What if they find out I'm still bleeding inside?
Leaking pain and anguish no bandaid or torniquet could vanquish.
But they don't let go.
So neither do you.
Your mind runs in circles.
Broken. Worthless.
Beyond repair.
Not enough or worth it. But those are lies.
You know they are but your body still believes them, feels them like
a weight crushing on your chest. EEERRRRAAAHHHHHHH!
You *want* this rest.
To lay down the weight and be *here*.
You want the tightness to disappear.
For the familiar fear to stop being a default
and resolve to trust the inherent goodness inside of all creatures.
Even though evil
is just as possible.
You reach for her and pull. Cross the void closer. Her head is yours
that you stroke, sweep away your hair from her face. Silence stills all time
in this moment in space.
Warmth envelopes our lines melding together.
My body wound up cries for relief.
Let,

go.

All these beliefs you've let live in us for too long. It's been long enough, we're done. Let go of the hate of yourself- that it's too late

to change the reality of events that happened. You can't undo the assault to us or your soul. But you can't go on living through the shame of feeling dirty or the blame

for being in the wrong place at the wrong time.

Or the relief of hopelessness that lets you drown in a sea of numb motionlessness.

That's too easy. We are your cells, your body

and we won't let you slip away in anonymity.

Feel her skin and remember.

This

is

good.

You don't have to winter this life so frozen.

You don't have to believe you were chosen

for suffering.

There's nothing wrong with you.

Let those who know you sing the song in your heart that you've so long forgotten.

Let the deadness be rotten and fall away.

Expose your soul again,

one embrace at a time. Heal your tension,

tear out the misconceptions that you are anything but exactly as you are - perfectly a mess

that noone,

especially you, should feel guilty about.

Let go, cherished one.

You can't hold the lies and us.

Give them up

so you can hug her closer.

She's waiting patiently for you to choose.
The only thing you have to lose
is an identity that was
never
actually
true.

PARENTAL JOY (for Ibrahim and Emily)

There is something infinitely
    intimate
    about a father holding his little girl. Like
    the love of the universe could unfurl
    in the closeness of the touch.
    Like their hugs
    can't be close or long enough. Like her eyes
    can't be brighter
    because she knows her dad is a fighter
    for her heart, her health, her joy.
    When the mother
    picks up her little boy, her gentleness
    whispers...
    of a mystery revealed only in knowing
    how he felt-
    safe and protected and cherished
    in her womb.
    Birth was just an opening of the tomb
    of separation, so she
    could wrap her arms around him
    tighter in her lap.
    When they tuck them in for a nap,
    when they ask their children for help,
    teach them how to pray,
    listen to what they have to say,
    are proud of them as they play, I wonder.
    How long does it take to fall in love?
    Or was it always there?

Waiting for us to stare at the intensity, and care Love wants to give.

When I see my friends parenting their kids, there's no lid to the wells

of attention,

intention,

emotion,

patience

and depth in their hearts.

I start to question, what's different?

What prevents other mothers and fathers

from living so fearlessly, in their roles

as guardians

of their offspring's souls, until they are old enough to champion

themselves.

My hope is that God will free all parents

from the hell

of ever believing

they are not enough as they are.

So they can give their children

all the peace and safety they have

and all the hope they don't

have guaranteed.

May we reach into the springs

that aren't rooted in ourselves

so we can give

and behold

The infinite love. May we never stop

Searching for ways

To never give up

On a better life

For everyone.

LOVE IS (for Jess and Michelle)

Love is patient, love is kind, unless they didn't do the dishes.

Love doesn't envy, love is pride, love respects your wishes.

Love is a mushroom, love is a frog, love is unafraid to show the world.

Love is alive, love changes, love lets the woman unfurl.

Love is tall, love is fun-sized, love leaves things on the bottom shelf.

Love is waiting, love is here, love found you a week after you found yourself.

Love is fun, love is daring, love wants to make sure you're impressed.

Love is gentle, love is caring, love bought you your first dress.

Love is service, love is Americorp, love is generous to others.

Love is fashion, love is joy, love is glad to look like her mother.

Love is a kiss, love is a hug, love is your hand in mine.

Love is primal, love is a pull, love is a lifeline.

Love is bright, love is excited, love rejoices this journey you start.

Love is brave, love is wild. May it grow til death do you part.

Love is honest, love values integrity, love cultivates a garden of life.

Love is trans, love is nonbinary. Love can't stop looking at their wife.

Love is friends, love is family. Our lives are better with you both around.

Love never fails, so congratulations, Mrs. & Mx. Hamilton-Brown.

STARING

You know when a problem has a face?
    It's not just something out of place,
    not another game to beat.
    It's a person. Being seen clearly in their defeat.
    It's the constant apologizing
    for existing
    in a space that's inconvenient for the public.
    But that piece of sidewalk was home last night. This morning they're
moving, constantly moving again.
    My hands get cold inside. He must be frozen
    out there.
    He said he had heart failure.
    What if he did? What if he wasn't lying?
    Why was that my first instinct, that he was not telling the truth?
    What if the person in front of me
    was actively trying
    to get their life in a safer state? Could today
    be the day he finds a break?
    I don't even know his name. All I gave him was a cup of coffee, while
politely asking if he would move away from the door.
    So others wouldn't see and be afraid.
    So no one would call the cops and take him
    to a different place.
    So they wouldn't have to avoid the most direct way into the building.
As if our comfort
    were worth his suffering.
    I want to know his story, truly, from his own mouth. I want to figure
out
    what got him here and if there's a way out.

I want to go with him to the shelter and introduce him to help I cannot give, praying he'll take it.

But all I can do is wait to get off from work.

I doubt he'll be there by then.

When did it become acceptable

to see another human on the ground

and keep going?

What have we found that's worth knowing

that countless starve,

overdose,

sell themselves,

are sold forcefully,

trying to make ends meet

and we...keep... walking.

Can we ban together to stop talking about homelessness and start doing something about the systems that make it possible?

Is it plausible to say that any minute, any day, that could happen to us,

as if we are different.

That could happen to *me*.

That could happen to *you*.

When do we choose complacent apathy

so we aren't disturbed by the memories

of tent cities,

dirty needles,

begging for

anything helps, on street corners.

Where are the borders between me

and *that* human?

Why is it acceptable- the distance I kept

from a man wrapped in a sleeping bag and out of his mind? When is it okay to 'put down'

our animals who have no voice anymore.
Why are hurting, broken, misunderstood people
a chore that others reluctantly give food
or a few dollars to?
That. Is. Enough.
I've had it with societies' lack of love and decency towards our
brothers and sisters-
Who are real human beings.
I'm just as guilty
for not having a clue what to do
or how to help.
So can we just agree that others are important. That we aren't free
until everyone is.
To not look away from the face
staring back at you.
To smile when you don't know what else to do.
To wonder why and
STOP JUDGING
what you don't know.
Let's go to the kindest parts of our hearts
and let it hurt.
Feel the wrongness of instinctual hate
or quickly walking away.
Don't add to the shame by making someone unworthy of your gaze.
Stay uncomfortable.
You'll never find a way to care if you don't try.
Don't become a burden to humanity
by trading your heart for heavy machinery.
We need to *feel* compassion.
Let's not ration our care
for blindness.
May we bare the ache

of our hands unable to steal their pain
so that one day, we won't just feel empathy
or angry-
we will heal the face
staring back at me.

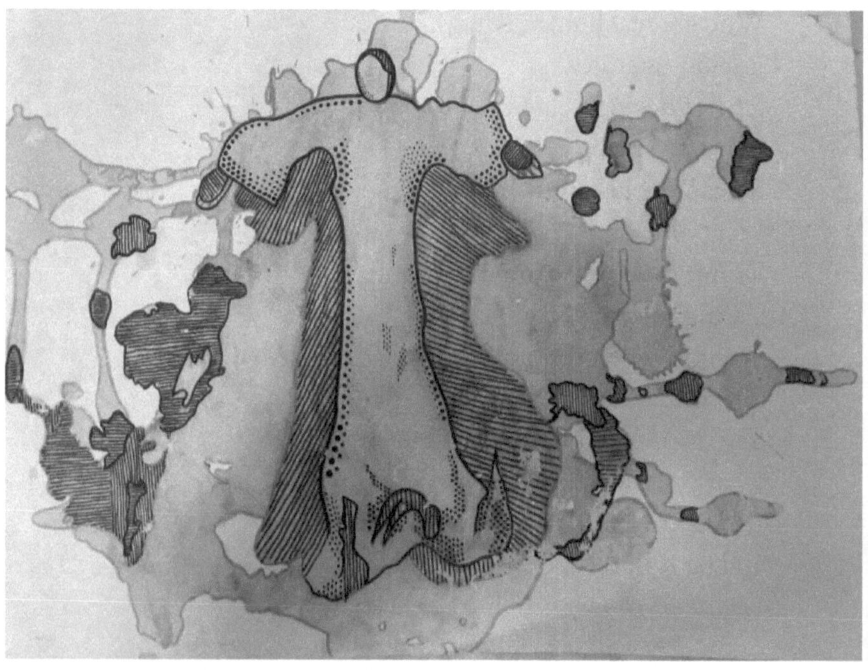

EDGES

The edges
    That shape us
    Are Sharp
    Pointy
    Smooth
    Long
    Round
    Short
    And can be found
    In absolutely everything
    We have ever experienced.
    Life is not a bunch of individual
    Moments.
    Life is a bunch of times
    We have tested
    Our piece of the puzzle
    Against others.
    Sometimes
    Our lines line up perfectly.
    Others we would have to cut
    Ours to fit
    Or
    Find another place to be.
    Which is not the worst solution.
    Edges serve as boundaries.
    The ones we cross
    We knew we shouldn't.
    The ones we never will
    Because it would take
    Too much of us.

The ones we never made because
We knew they
Would not be able to stay behind them.
Edges define us.
Like the contours of our face
Our bodies.
The hands of the ones
You know most intimately.
Edges invite the joining
Of energy,
Love,
Serendipity,
Hugs.
The kind you never have
To pull away from.
Whenever you come across
An edge,
Don't think of it as separation
Between you and me.
Think of it as the invitation
To breatheeeeeeee
The same air.
To see the same landscapes.
To wonder the same thoughts.
To grow closer
Regardless of how far away you might be.
Edges remind us
That though we are human
For a little while,
We are all connected.
Edges are just the reminders
That we one day

Will not be apart.
We will all be
home.

CHOOSE

There is a stubbornness about suffering.
That in our blundering, clumsy wondering
whether someday we'll get to where we're going, we refuse to look
from the path right under our feet.
We are told incessantly, like the bleating of sheep, to keep going.
Keep walking.
Follow the leader, Swallow the expectation.
Go to the pre planned destination.
That, is... your life.
And in our stubbornness we trudge along,
fighting the mud that wants to suck us under.
It's exhausting. Nevermind what it's costing
our souls.

But
there were sages of old
who dared to stop for a moment.
To breathe in, hold it, breathe out, and look up. They blinked as they
tried to open their eyes wider.
"Look, at, those, stars?!" They cried. "Look at the wonderful sight!
It's beautiful."
Those around them kept walking,
brushed them to the side and sighed.
"Why don't you look up with me?" They begged. Those walking just
shook their heads. One stopped.
"Why would I? I need to keep going. Or
someone else will take my spot that will become open. Why did *you*
stop? Can't you see

the line is broken? You are selfish for taking this moment."
And they kept walking.
The looker stopped talking.
How could they say such a thing?!
Why was following this even worth anything?
The stars continued to sparkle and one could almost hear them sing...
"Can you see the sky calling from the sea of stars above? Can you know that there is more for you- warmth and hope and love? Do you know that you are not so small, standing by yourself? Look up, dear one, look up."
So they kept looking and kept searching.
What they found was horrifying. They were not
on a path,
they were in a circle, digging
a hole deeper with all the following.
They were not working to
somewhere,
they were in a fence.
This made no sense!
Where were the accomplishments?
Where was the end?
And then. They saw something.
More footprints.
Tracks that left the circle. So they followed them.
At first they circled the walkers, then over the fence and around. They had spent most of the time around the posts. They kept following in hopes that maybe,
just maybe,
there would be someone else at the end.
The steps led to a road.
They ran, throwing arms ahead, feeling alive. Looking for signs of another life.

First they saw light,

then smoke rising from the chimney of a house.

A small light bobbed in the distance and slowly got bigger. They didn't know what this could mean so they slowed, stopping at a sign hung between two posts.

Confused, they stared at it. Compared the words they had seen before but couldn't place its meaning. The light became bright and connected seemingly to another

human

being. They crashed into them. Embracing, holding,

squeezing

the person between their arms.

"Who are you? And what is that farm everyone is stuck inside?" The other gasping, sweating, smiling, laughing.

"I am Friend! It's so good to see you. I'm so glad you found your way here. That is the herd of achievement. There are many other herds-bereavement, conceit, anger, fear, isolation. But you are here!"

"Where is here? Are you alone? And what does that sign say?"

Friend took a deep breath and laughed.

"Here is called, Home. It's the best. You're going to love it. And that sign says, REST."

"Wow," they said. "Do I have to go back

to the herd? Can I stay here?" Friend nodded.

"Stay as long as you will. As for the herds,

it's your choice where you live. It's really up to you.

What do you have to lose? The freedom is yours to choose."

Don't miss out!

Visit the website below and you can sign up to receive emails whenever Savanah Stone publishes a new book. There's no charge and no obligation.

https://books2read.com/r/B-A-YANV-RGECC

BOOKS2READ

Connecting independent readers to independent writers.

About the Author

Hi! I'm Savanah Stone.

I'm a creative looking to propagate love and light in any way I can. Here's a bit of the reasons behind my poems:

I grew up in church and spent five years as a youth pastor before transitioning into a year and a half working in mental health - trauma care. Along with these vocations I was married three years before getting divorced three days before Covid-19. During the pandemic my partner relapsed three times from alcoholism. I have personally experienced the realities of depression, anxiety, abuse, and trauma and I'm still moving forward. The beautiful thing about words is they don't judge you. I'm thankful for the healing I receive through them.

I'm currently living in Asheville, NC loving the mountains and assisting inside Second Wins's - The Nerd Dungeon! My next creative project is a fantasy series called - The Phoenix Trilogy! Can't wait to share it with you! - Sav